I0122718

Eulogies

When

Accidental Death

Takes Our Beloved:

Writing Guidelines, Examples and Templates

With Tips for Grieving, Healing and Moving On

J Jordan

Notable+

Copyright & Disclaimer

EULOGIES WHEN ACCIDENTAL DEATH TAKES OUR BELOVED: WRITING GUIDELINES, EXAMPLES AND TEMPLATES

The author, J Jordan, is represented by Notable Plus LLC, Palm Bay, Florida.

Eulogies When Accidental Death Takes Our Beloved: Writing Guidelines, Examples and Templates
Paperback: 129 Pages
Print Quality: Black ink and 55# (90 GSM) cream paper
ISBN-10: 1-960176-16-1
ISBN-13: 978-1-960176-16-5

Notable+ also publishes its books and content in a variety of electronic formats and online. Some of the content that appears in print may not be available in electronic books or online and some of the content that appears online or in electronic formats may not be available in print.

Contents

Preface

Firstly, please accept my deepest condolences. Losing a loved one is an incredibly challenging experience, and I sincerely pray that you find the strength to endure during this time of immense pain and loss.

Losing a loved one is an incredibly challenging experience, and when it occurs unexpectedly due to an accident, the shock and grief can be even more overwhelming. However, amidst the sorrow, it is crucial to remember that our loved ones had a unique journey that deserves to be celebrated. By honoring their life, we can find solace in the cherished memories they left behind and keep their spirit alive within our hearts.

Within the pages of this book, we offer a collection of example eulogies tailored specifically for those who have lost loved ones in accidental circumstances. Whether it be vehicular accidents, fire-related incidents, drug overdoses, drownings, falls, or other generic accidents, we provide heartfelt eulogies to guide you through this difficult time. Furthermore, we present a step-by-step approach to assist you in crafting and delivering a meaningful eulogy. Additionally, we address frequently asked questions that encompass various aspects of eulogy writing, such as dealing with memories, coping with grief, and finding the strength to move forward.

This book has been meticulously designed to provide you with the necessary tools to navigate the process of writing, delivering, and coping with the tumultuous emotions that accompany such a challenging period. Our ultimate goal is not only to help you create and deliver a fitting eulogy, but also to empower you to progress through the stages of grief and ultimately find healing and the ability to move forward.

When news of the passing of a loved one arrives, and you find yourself overwhelmed with emotions while simultaneously planning the funeral and holding the rest of the family together, writing a eulogy becomes an arduous task. The raw and gut-wrenching thoughts of your loved one being gone make it challenging to create a eulogy that truly honors their memory. Moreover, amidst all the chaos, you must gather the courage to stand before a grieving audience, paying tribute to the deceased and offering words of encouragement to those in mourning. The weight of this responsibility can feel like an additional burden atop the mountain of challenges you already face.

However, it is a task that must be undertaken, and if you are reading this, it means that this great responsibility has been entrusted to you. I have personally experienced the position you find yourself in right now, and I wholeheartedly empathize with your situation. Despite the overwhelming emotions you may be experiencing, I firmly believe that you possess bravery and courage, even if you may not feel it at this moment.

The eulogy is a unique and distinct type of speech that requires a different approach due to many factors, including the mental and emotional state of the audience. This book is specifically designed to assist you in this particular task. It is not a generic speech writing guide, as that is not what you need at this moment. My intention is not to delve into the mechanics of speech writing, but rather to provide you with specific wording, examples and templates that you can adapt, replicate and use to craft your tribute or at least inspire and guide your eulogy writing process.

The body of the eulogy contains crucial sections that we have provided for your convenience. These sections can be customized to suit your specific requirements. Within the eulogies presented in this book, you will find introductions, conclusions, and segments dedicated to sharing cherished memories, highlighting the deceased's passions, discussing their influence, and offering words of comfort to those attending the funeral.

Eulogies employ specific language and sections that enable us to effectively convey the sentiments we wish to express. During challenging times, it can be difficult to find the right words and establish a structure that effectively communicates our emotions while paying tribute to someone who held great significance in our lives.

This book also serves as a guide to help you navigate the grieving process while providing examples and templates for eulogy writing. You can largely copy, modify, and adapt these resources to suit the eulogy you are preparing. Its purpose is to alleviate some of the difficulties associated with this task during such a challenging time.

While these eulogies can serve as sources of inspiration, it is important to personalize your tribute to reflect the unique life and relationship you shared with your loved one. Use the structure and themes highlighted here as guides, but make sure to incorporate your own memories, anecdotes, and emotions to create a heartfelt eulogy that truly honors your loved one.

About Sections, Fields, FAQ and More

Eulogy Sections

This book offers a variety of sections that you can customize and incorporate into your eulogy. The language used in these sections is in line with the common expressions found in eulogies. By eliminating the need to fret over the wording or search for the perfect phrases to express your emotions, writing eulogies becomes a less daunting task.

Fields

We have incorporated specific fields, such as [Name], to conveniently accommodate the inclusion of relevant information about the departed individual. These fields greatly assist in tailoring the eulogies to honor your loved one in a personalized manner.

Tips

Italicized tips are a valuable component designed to ignite creativity and motivation within your writing endeavors. These carefully curated suggestions serve as a catalyst for inspiration, encouraging innovative thinking and the exploration of new ideas.

Prompts

These words serve as a compass for your writing endeavors, urging you to include captivating stories, cherished memories, and entertaining anecdotes.

FAQ

Our Frequently Asked Questions (FAQ) section provides comprehensive answers to common inquiries regarding writing eulogies, as well as coping with loss, healing, and moving forward.

Once again, we extend our deepest condolences to you and your loved ones during this time of need. We sincerely pray that you find the strength to carry on.

1. Writing Eulogies for Loved Ones Whose Journey Ended Abruptly

1.1 Reflecting on a Life of Purpose and Passion

In every person's journey, there are those exceptional souls whose lives are marked by an unwavering sense of purpose and an infectious passion for making a difference. Unfortunately, life can sometimes take an unexpected turn, abruptly bringing an end to their remarkable presence. In these moments, writing a eulogy becomes not only an act of remembrance but also a celebration of a life full of purpose and passion. The following chapters aim to guide you through the process of crafting a eulogy for such an inspirational being, offering insights on sharing their journey, gathering meaningful memories, honoring their achievements, navigating the emotions of grief, and ultimately delivering a tribute that leaves a lasting legacy.

2. Top Causes of Accidental Death

2.1 Introduction to Accidental Deaths

Accidental deaths are a tragic reality that impact countless lives every year. From motor vehicle accidents to unintentional poisonings, falls, drownings, fires, and more, these incidents claim lives and leave families devastated. In this section, we delve into the top causes of accidental deaths, shedding light on the underlying factors, and exploring ways to pay tribute to the lives lost to accidental deaths. By understanding the leading causes of accidental deaths, we can create a tribute that leaves a memorable legacy and honors our loved one.

2.2 Motor Vehicle Accidents

When it comes to accidental deaths, motor vehicle accidents rank high on the list. Losing a loved one is never easy, but when it happens suddenly and unexpectedly due to a vehicular tragedy, the grief can be particularly overwhelming. The shock and trauma of such a loss can leave families feeling disoriented and emotionally raw. The suddenness of the accident can make it difficult to process and accept the reality of the situation. It's important to recognize and validate the unique challenges and emotions that families face in these circumstances.

2.3 Unintentional Poisoning

Unintentional poisoning is a significant cause of accidental deaths that often goes unnoticed. The loss of a loved one is an irrevocable tragedy that can shake the very foundation of our lives. When that loss is due to poisoning, it carries an additional layer of complexity and anguish. Coping with the loss of a loved one due to poisoning is a deeply personal journey, filled with unique challenges and emotions.

2.4 Falls and Injuries

Falls and injuries account for a significant number of accidental deaths, particularly among the elderly. As we age, our physical capabilities may decline, making us more susceptible to falls.

Losing a loved one in a tragic accident, such as an accidental fall, can be an incredibly difficult and painful experience. As we navigate the depths of grief, it becomes essential to honor the memory of our loved one by cherishing their achievements and contributions. Though we may delve into the circumstances surrounding the fatal fall, we must not dwell there, instead, we should seek understanding and closure.

2.5 Drowning and Water-Related Accidents

The passing of a loved one is always a deeply painful and challenging experience. It is especially harrowing when their life was tragically cut short due to a drowning accident. However, amidst the sorrow and heartache, it is crucial to honor and celebrate the beautiful life they lived. It can be a difficult task to deliver a heartfelt tribute to a loved one who touched the lives of many. Through exploring their early life, accomplishments, cherished memories, and the lessons we can glean from their untimely passing, we aim to keep their spirit alive and inspire others to embrace life and advocate for water safety.

2.6 Fire and Burns

When a devastating house fire claims the lives of loved ones, the profound impact of the loss can be overwhelming. Eulogies provide a space for collective mourning, allowing us to honor and remember the individuals who have left us, while also finding solace in shared memories and stories. This book explores the significance of eulogies in the wake of a house fire tragedy, providing insights on writing and delivering meaningful eulogies, highlighting the importance of community support, and offering guidance on navigating the complex journey of grief and mourning. By embracing the power of eulogies, we can find hope, love, and resilience amidst the darkest of times.

2.7 Accidental Overdose and Substance Abuse: The Growing Epidemic

Eulogies serve as a profound means to remember and pay tribute to those who have tragically succumbed to the ravages of drug addiction.

The opioid crisis has become a prevalent issue in the United States, with numerous cases of accidental overdose stemming from the misuse of prescription medications.

Illicit drugs, such as heroin and cocaine, continue to pose a serious threat to individuals and communities.

However, when we lose a loved one to substance abuse we must remember that each individual's story is unique, and through the art of eulogizing, we can celebrate their lives, commemorate their accomplishments, and reflect upon the challenges they faced.

2.8 Conclusion

Accidental deaths are profound losses that touch families, friends, and communities alike. This book explores the significance of sharing memories through eulogies for those lost to accident and tragedy. It delves into understanding the impact of accidental death and coping with grief. Furthermore, we emphasize the importance of prevention and delve into the power of eulogies in inspiring change and advocacy. By shedding light on these personal narratives, we can foster compassion, empathy, and hope in the face of accidental death.

3. Understanding the Power of Eulogies

3.1 A Powerful Expression of Love

When we gather to honor the life of someone special, a eulogy becomes a powerful tool for expressing our love, admiration, and appreciation. It is a chance to reflect on a life that was lived with purpose and passion, and to celebrate the impact they had on our lives and the world around them.

But let's not take the task of writing a eulogy too seriously. Yes, it is a somber occasion, but it's also an opportunity to remember the joyful moments and funny anecdotes that made this person unique. So, let's approach this task with a mix of reverence and lightheartedness, honoring their memory in a way that captures their essence.

3.2 Capturing the Essence: Understanding the Inspirational Journey

To truly capture the essence of the person we are eulogizing, we need to delve into their life philosophy and the core values that guided their actions. What were their beliefs, passions, and dreams? Did they have a motto they lived by? Understanding these aspects will help us shape a eulogy that reflects who they were.

Additionally, tracing the significant milestones and transformative experiences in their life will provide valuable insights. It could be the time they overcame a great challenge, achieved a personal goal, or discovered their true calling. These moments shaped them and deserve to be acknowledged.

3.3 Gathering Memories: Sharing Personal Anecdotes and Stories

When we gather to celebrate a life, it becomes a shared experience of remembrance and reflection. As the eulogist, it's important to involve family and friends in the process. Invite them to share their personal anecdotes and stories, as they often hold precious memories that give a fuller picture of who this person was.

As you gather these stories, take the time to organize and categorize them. Create a timeline or themes that align with the different aspects of their life or their personality. This will help you structure your eulogy and ensure that you touch upon the highlights that truly capture their spirit.

3.4 Honoring Achievements: Highlighting Accomplishments and Contributions

In the eulogy, it's important to give due recognition to the achievements and contributions of the person being honored. Whether they excelled in their profession, achieved personal goals, or made a positive impact within their community, these accomplishments deserve acknowledgment.

Highlighting their contributions to the community and society will help everyone present appreciate the positive mark they left on the world. It could be their involvement in charity work, mentorship, or advocacy for important causes. By showcasing their impact, we inspire others to follow in their footsteps and continue their legacy.

Writing a eulogy is not an easy task, but it is an opportunity to celebrate a life lived to the fullest. So, let's embrace this responsibility with empathy, love, and a touch of humor, ensuring that the memories we share honor the person's unique journey and the lasting impact they had on our lives.

3.5 Embracing Emotions: Navigating Grief

Grief is a powerful emotion that can hit us unexpectedly and leave us feeling lost and overwhelmed. When writing a eulogy, it's important to acknowledge and embrace these feelings. Allow yourself the space to mourn, to cry, and to experience the pain of loss. It's through this process of grieving that we can ultimately find solace and healing.

Reach out to friends, family, or support groups who can provide comfort and understanding during this challenging time. Share stories and memories together, laugh and cry together, and find strength in the shared love for the person who has passed. Remember, you don't have to navigate grief alone.

3.6 Celebrating the Joyful Aspects of the Individual's Life

While grief is an integral part of the mourning process, it's equally important to celebrate the life and accomplishments of the person we've lost. Think back to the moments of joy and laughter shared with them, the moments of inspiration they provided, and the impact they had on the lives of others.

Whether it was their unwavering kindness, their infectious laughter, or their unwavering determination, find ways to celebrate the qualities that made them special. Share these moments in the eulogy, reminding everyone of the light that this person brought into the world. By focusing on the positive aspects of their life, we can honor their memory and keep their spirit alive.

4. Crafting the Eulogy: A Step-by-Step Guide to Writing a Meaningful Tribute

4.1 Understanding the Purpose and Structure of a Eulogy

A eulogy serves as a heartfelt tribute to the person who has passed away. It's an opportunity to reflect on their life, share memories, and celebrate their accomplishments. Understanding the purpose of a eulogy is key to crafting a meaningful tribute.

The structure of a eulogy typically includes an introduction, where you establish your connection to the person and set the tone for the speech. Then, you can delve into different aspects of their life – childhood, achievements, relationships, and so on. Finally, conclude the eulogy by summarizing the impact they had on others and expressing gratitude for the time shared together.

4.2 Gathering Information and Personal Reflections

When writing a eulogy, it's helpful to gather information from various sources: family members, friends, colleagues, and even the person's own writings or speeches. Listen to the stories and anecdotes they share, and reflect on your own personal experiences with the individual.

Take time to recollect specific moments, conversations, or actions that truly exemplify who they were. These personal reflections will add depth and authenticity to your eulogy. Remember, it's not just about listing achievements or accolades – it's about capturing the essence of the person and sharing it with others.

4.3 Organizing and Crafting the Eulogy with Care

With the gathered information and personal reflections in hand, it's time to organize and craft your eulogy. Begin by creating an outline, highlighting the key themes or aspects you want to cover. Then, fill in the details and connect them in a way that flows naturally.

While it's important to be concise, don't be afraid to inject humor or share personal anecdotes that will resonate with the audience. You want the eulogy to feel authentic and true to the person you are honoring. Remember, it's not about impressing others with your writing skills; it's about expressing genuine emotions and capturing the essence of the person's life.

4.4 Conclusion: Leaving a Lasting Legacy and Finding Closure

4.4.1 Reflecting on the Individual's Impact and Legacy

As you bring your eulogy to a close, take a moment to reflect on the person's impact and legacy. Consider the ways in which they touched the lives of others, the positive change they brought to their community, and the lasting memories they created.

Their legacy is not just about the achievements or titles they held, but about the lasting impressions they made on the hearts and minds of those they encountered. By honoring and acknowledging this impact, you help to ensure that their memory lives on.

4.4.2 Finding Closure and Moving Forward with Inspiration

Writing and delivering a eulogy is a cathartic process that allows us to find closure and begin the healing journey. As you conclude your eulogy, remember to offer words of comfort and strength to those in attendance. Share your own commitment to carry forward the values and lessons learned from the person you've lost, finding inspiration in their life to guide you on your own path.

Though the journey may be bittersweet, by celebrating a life full of purpose and passion, we can find solace in knowing that our loved one's memory will continue to inspire us and others for years to come.

4.5 Conclusion: A Celebration of Life

As we conclude the journey of celebrating a life full of purpose and passion, be reminded of the profound impact one individual can have on the world. Through the process of writing a eulogy, we honor their accomplishments, share cherished memories, and embrace the emotions that come with loss. By delivering a heartfelt tribute, we ensure that their legacy lives on, inspiring others to follow their example of living with purpose and passion. May this act of remembrance bring us closure, while reminding us to seize each day with intention and make a difference in the lives of those around us.

5. Delivering the Eulogy: Tips for Public Speaking and Connecting with the Audience

5.1 Preparing for the Emotional Challenge of Public Speaking

Public speaking can be an emotional challenge, especially when delivering a eulogy. Take the time to prepare yourself mentally and emotionally before stepping up to the podium. Practice reading the eulogy out loud, allowing yourself to become comfortable with the words and emotions associated with them.

If you feel overwhelmed during the delivery, take deep breaths and remind yourself of the love and admiration you have for the person you are honoring. Embrace the vulnerability of the moment, knowing that sharing your feelings will help others in their own grieving process.

5.2 Engaging the Audience and Establishing a Connection

When delivering a eulogy, it's important to establish a connection with the audience. Speak from the heart, make eye contact, and use body language to convey your emotions. Engage the audience by sharing relatable stories or inviting them to participate in a moment of reflection or remembrance.

Remember, the eulogy is not just for you—it's an opportunity to bring people together, to uplift their spirits, and to honor the person's memory as a collective group. By creating a sense of connection, you can help others find solace, inspiration, and comfort during this difficult time.

5.3 Leaving a Lasting Legacy through Words

Crafting and delivering a meaningful eulogy is an opportunity to leave a lasting legacy for your loved one. By choosing your words carefully and sharing heartfelt sentiments, you can honor their life and create a lasting impact on those who hear your tribute. Remember that the power of a eulogy lies not only in the memories it evokes but also in the comfort and solace it provides to those who are grieving. Embrace this chance to celebrate a life well-lived and give your loved one a meaningful send-off.

6. Finding Peace Amidst Loss: Crafting Comforting and Healing Eulogies for Families Affected by Vehicular Tragedy

Losing a loved one in a vehicular tragedy is a devastating experience that leaves families grappling with unique and overwhelming grief. In the midst of such pain and loss, the task of crafting a eulogy can seem both daunting and essential. A well-crafted eulogy has the power to honor the life and legacy of the deceased, provide comfort to the grieving family, and offer a path towards healing. This chapter aims to guide and support individuals in writing comforting and healing eulogies for families affected by vehicular tragedy. By understanding the specific challenges of this type of loss and employing meaningful strategies, we can help bring solace and peace to those who are mourning.

6.1 Understanding the Unique Grief of Families Affected by Vehicular Tragedy

6.1.1 The Impact of Sudden and Traumatic Loss

Losing a loved one is never easy, but when it happens suddenly and unexpectedly due to a vehicular tragedy, the grief can be particularly overwhelming. The shock and trauma of such a loss can leave families feeling disoriented and emotionally raw. The suddenness of the accident can make it difficult to process and accept the reality of the situation. It's important to recognize and validate the unique challenges and emotions that families face in these circumstances.

6.1.2 Navigating the Complex Emotions and Challenges of Vehicular Tragedy

Vehicular tragedies often involve not only the loss of a loved one but also the involvement of other parties, such as reckless drivers or drunk drivers. This can intensify the anger, frustration, and confusion that families experience during the grieving process. Additionally, families may have to deal with legal proceedings, insurance claims, or media attention, adding even more stress to an already difficult situation. Understanding and acknowledging these complex emotions and challenges can help in providing the necessary support and compassion to affected families.

6.2 Crafting Eulogies that Reflect the Life and Legacy of the Deceased

6.2.1 Gathering Information and Stories about the Deceased

To create a meaningful and personalized eulogy, it's important to gather as much information and stories as possible about the deceased. Reach out to family members, friends, and colleagues who can share anecdotes, memories, and achievements. Every person has a unique story, and by collecting these narratives, you can paint a vivid picture of the person's life, personality, and passions.

6.2.2 Highlighting Significant Achievements and Contributions

While it's important to capture the essence of the person's life, don't forget to focus on their accomplishments and contributions as well. Whether it's professional achievements, community involvement, or acts of kindness, highlighting these aspects can help create a eulogy that reflects the positive impact the person had on the world. Celebrating their life and the mark they left behind can bring comfort and solace to grieving families.

6.3 The Power of Words: Choosing the Right Tone and Language

6.3.1 Striking a Balance between Grief and Celebration

Crafting a eulogy requires delicately balancing the grief and loss felt by the family with the celebration of the person's life. It's important to acknowledge the pain and sadness while also emphasizing the joy and love that the person brought into the lives of others. By finding this balance, the eulogy can provide a sense of comfort and healing amidst the sorrow.

6.3.2 Avoiding Clichés and Generic Phrases

When writing a eulogy, it's crucial to avoid using clichés or generic phrases that may come across as insincere. Instead, strive for authenticity and originality. Speak from the heart, using language that is personal and genuine. Be yourself and let your words reflect the unique relationship you had with the person who passed away. This will ensure that the eulogy resonates with the audience in a meaningful way.

6.4 Incorporating Personal Stories and Memories in Eulogies

6.4.1 Encouraging Family and Friends to Share Meaningful Anecdotes

To make the eulogy more personal and relatable, encourage family and friends to share their own stories and anecdotes about the deceased. These personal perspectives can add depth and richness to the eulogy, showing different facets of the person's character and the impact they had on those around them.

6.4.2 Weaving Personal Stories into the Eulogy Narrative

Once you have gathered these personal stories, find ways to incorporate them into the eulogy narrative. Intertwine these anecdotes with key moments and themes that capture the essence of the person's life. This will create a eulogy that is not only a reflection of who they were but also a source of comfort and connection for grieving families.

6.5 Providing Comfort and Support through Meaningful Quotes and Scriptures

6.5.1 Selecting Quotes and Scriptures that Resonate with the Deceased's Beliefs or Values

When it comes to offering comfort through quotes and scriptures in a eulogy, it's important to keep the departed loved one in mind. Think about their beliefs, values, and the things they held dear. Did they have a favorite quote or a verse from their favorite scripture? Incorporating these into the eulogy can be a beautiful way to honor their memory and provide solace to those in attendance.

Think about it this way: if the person was a free-spirited adventurer, you might consider a quote like, "Life is either a daring adventure or nothing at all" by Helen Keller. Or, if they found solace in religious teachings, you might draw from a comforting scripture that speaks to their faith.

6.5.2 Using Quotes and Scriptures to Offer Hope and Encouragement

Quotes and scriptures have a way of touching our hearts and offering comfort during difficult times. When crafting a eulogy for families affected by vehicular tragedy, it's essential to weave in quotes and scriptures that offer hope and encouragement.

These words can provide a glimmer of light in the darkest of times, reminding everyone that even in grief, there is room for healing and growth. Quotes like Maya Angelou's, "You may encounter many defeats, but you must not be defeated," or scriptures like Psalm 34:18, "The Lord is close to the brokenhearted and saves those who are crushed in spirit," can serve as reminders that there is always hope and strength to be found.

6.6 Acknowledging the Impact of Vehicular Tragedy and Offering Words of Hope

6.6.1 Addressing the Tragic Circumstances with Sensitivity

Vehicular tragedies are heart-wrenching and often leave families grappling with a range of emotions. It's important to address the circumstances with sensitivity, acknowledging the pain and loss experienced by the family.

Instead of dwelling on the details of the tragedy, focus on expressing empathy and compassion. Let the family know that you are there to support them through this difficult time. A simple phrase like, "Words cannot express the depth of pain we feel for your loss," can go a long way in offering comfort.

6.6.2 Sharing Words of Hope and Resilience in the Face of Adversity

In the face of tragedy, it's crucial to offer words of hope and resilience to help families find strength amidst their sorrow. Share stories or anecdotes that highlight the deceased's ability to overcome challenges or their unwavering spirit.

Encourage the family to remember their loved one's legacy and the impact they had on others, emphasizing that their memory will live on through the stories, lessons, and love they left behind. In times of darkness, reminding families of the power of love, community, and the human spirit can bring a glimmer of light to their hearts.

6.7 Saying the Final Goodbye

As we navigate the difficult process of saying goodbye to loved ones affected by vehicular tragedy, crafting a comforting and healing eulogy becomes an act of love and remembrance. By understanding the unique grief experienced by these families, selecting the right words and tone, incorporating personal stories, and offering words of hope, we can provide the support and solace they need during this challenging time. Through the power of eulogies, we can help these families find peace amidst their loss and honor the lives that were tragically taken from us.

7. Eulogy 1 - Eulogy for a Loved One Lost to Vehicular Accident

7.1 Introducing the Purpose of the Eulogy

7.1.1 Introductions and Greetings

As we gather here today, we come together with heavy hearts to remember and pay tribute to the life of [Name], a beloved individual who was tragically taken from us in a car accident. I am [Your Name], [Name]'s [Your relationship to the deceased] and I am honored to speak on behalf of the loved ones gathered here today to pay tribute. This eulogy serves as a heartfelt remembrance of the person we cherished, celebrating [his/her] remarkable life, and offering solace and support to one another during this challenging time. We gather not only to mourn our loss but also to honor [Name]'s memory and find strength in the love and memories we shared. Let us join together in reflection and celebration as we remember the impact this extraordinary person had on our lives.

7.1.2 The Loved Ones who Continue the Legacy

Our beloved [Name]'s passing has left a profound void in our lives. In reflecting on [his/her] life, it is important to acknowledge those who continue to carry on [his/her] legacy. [Name] is survived by [State and name the close kins e.g. [his/her] loving family, including [his/her] devoted [husband / wife], [Name], and their [number] children [List Names], who were the center of [his/her] universe.] [State and name other relatives e.g. [He/She] leaves behind a host of cherished relatives, including nieces, nephews, and cousins whom [he/she] held dear.] Additionally, [he/she] touched the lives of countless friends and acquaintances through [his/her] graciousness and unwavering support. [His/Her] presence will be greatly missed by all who had the privilege of knowing [him/her]. Although this loss brings immeasurable grief, we find solace in knowing that [Name] has engendered a lasting impact on those whose lives [he/she] gracefully enhanced with love and joy.

7.2 Reflecting on the Tragic Car Accident

7.2.1 Describing the Circumstances and Impact of the Car Accident

In a cruel twist of fate, our [Name]'s life was abruptly cut short by a tragic car accident. The circumstances surrounding this event have left us stunned and devastated. Such accidents remind us of the fragility of life and the unpredictable nature of the world we live in. Our hearts ache for the life and potential lost so suddenly.

7.2.2 Expressing Shock, Grief, and Initial Reactions

The news of the car accident struck us like a bolt of lightning, leaving us breathless and questioning how something so tragic could happen to someone so full of life. The initial shock quickly gave way to waves of grief, as we grappled with the unfathomable pain of loss. These emotions are overwhelming, but they are a testament to the deep love and connection we shared with our departed loved one, [Name].

7.3 Celebrating the Life and Achievements of the Departed

7.3.1 Recounting Our Loved One's Accomplishments and Contributions

While it is profoundly difficult to find solace amidst the sorrow, let us take a moment to celebrate the extraordinary life lived by our departed loved one. [Name] touched the lives of many, leaving an indelible mark on the world around [him/her]. From [his/her] career achievements to [his/her] personal triumphs, [his/her] legacy will continue to inspire and resonate within all those who knew them.

7.3.2 Highlighting the Positive Impact on Others' Lives

Our departed loved one had an uncanny ability to bring joy and light into the lives of others. Whether through [Name]'s compassionate nature, infectious laughter, or unwavering support, [he/she] made an immense impact on those fortunate enough to have crossed [his/her] path. [Name]'s generosity knew no bounds, and [he/she] left an imprint on our hearts that will forever remain.

7.4 Fond Memories and Personal Anecdotes

7.4.1 Sharing Heartfelt Stories and Memories of the Departed

As we navigate through this time of grief, let us cherish the memories we shared with our departed loved one. These cherished moments, often etched into the fabric of our lives, serve as a reminder of [his/her] spirit and essence. Through heartfelt stories and shared experiences, we keep [Name]'s memory alive, finding solace in the laughter and tears we once shared.

7.4.2 Illustrating the Loved One's Personality and Quirks

Our departed loved one possessed a unique personality that brought a spark to every room [he/she] entered. [Name]'s quirks and idiosyncrasies made [him/her] all the more endearing, creating memories that will forever bring a smile to our faces. From [his/her] contagious enthusiasm to [his/her] wicked sense of humor, we were blessed to have been a part of [Name]'s extraordinary journey.

Let us remember our departed loved one with love, laughter, and a deep appreciation for the time we shared. Though [Name]'s presence is no longer physical, [his/her] spirit lives on in each and every one of us. May we find comfort in the memories we hold dear and may [his/her] legacy forever inspire us to embrace life with the same passion and zest [he/she] embodied.

7.5 The Impact of the Loss on Family and Friends

7.5.1 Addressing the Emotional Toll on Immediate Family

Losing a loved one in a car accident is an unimaginable tragedy that shakes the foundation of any family. The emotional toll it takes on immediate family members cannot be easily put into words. The pain, grief, and sense of loss are overwhelming, leaving a void that can never be filled. In the midst of such heartbreak, it is important for family members to lean on one another for support, to share their feelings openly, and to find solace in the memories they hold dear.

7.5.2 Recognizing the Support and Unity of Friends and Extended Family

While immediate family members bear the brunt of the loss, the impact is felt by friends and extended family as well. In times of tragedy, the true strength of relationships becomes evident. Friends and extended family stand united, offering their unwavering support, love, and understanding. Their presence provides a sense of comfort and reminds us that we are not alone in our grief. Through their support, they help ease the burden and serve as a constant reminder that we are surrounded by people who care deeply. And so I say a heartfelt and special thanks to all who have provided support to the family and loved ones during this difficult time.

7.6 Coping with Grief and Finding Strength

7.6.1 Discussing the Stages of Grief and the Healing Process

Grief is a complex journey that everyone experiences differently. It is important to understand that grief does not follow a linear path but rather unfolds in stages. From denial and anger to bargaining, depression, and finally acceptance, each stage presents its own challenges and emotions. Healing takes time, and it is essential to allow oneself to process these emotions fully. Seeking support from grief counseling, support groups, or even confiding in a trusted friend can provide the guidance needed to navigate through the healing process.

7.6.2 Sharing Coping Mechanisms and Supportive Resources

In times of grief, finding healthy coping mechanisms is crucial. Engaging in activities that bring solace, such as journaling, practicing mindfulness, or expressing emotions through art, can provide a sense of release. Additionally, seeking out supportive resources, such as grief support hotlines, online forums, or grief retreats, can offer a safe space to share experiences with others who have gone through similar losses. Remember, finding strength in vulnerability and seeking support is not a sign of weakness but rather a testament to the resilience of the human spirit.

7.7 Lessons Learned and Road to Healing

7.7.1 Reflecting on the Lessons Drawn from the Tragedy

In the face of tragedy, there are valuable lessons that can be learned. It reminds us of the fragility and unpredictability of life, urging us to cherish every moment and prioritize what truly matters. It teaches us the importance of expressing our love and gratitude to those around us while we still can. It also serves as a reminder to be vigilant on the roads, advocating for safer driving practices and encouraging others to do the same. Through reflection, we can use these lessons to honor [Name]'s memory and prevent similar tragedies from happening in the future.

7.7.2 Emphasizing the Importance of Healing and Moving Forward

Healing is a personal journey, and there is no set timeline for moving forward. It is essential to honor the grief process while also embracing the possibility of healing. As time passes, it becomes important to focus on the positive memories, celebrating the life lived rather than the life lost. Embracing new beginnings and allowing oneself to find joy in life does not diminish the love for [Name] but rather honors [his/her] memory by living life to the fullest.

7.8 Final Thoughts: Honoring the Memory and Moving Forward

7.8.1 Paying Tribute to the Departed and Their Legacy

As we bid farewell to [Name], it is crucial to pay tribute to [his/her] memory and the impact [he/she] had on our lives. This may involve creating a memorial, sharing stories and anecdotes, or participating in activities that were near and dear to [his/her] heart. By keeping [Name]'s spirit alive, we ensure that [his/her] legacy continues to inspire and guide us.

7.8.2 Encouraging a Positive Outlook and Embracing Life's Journey

In the midst of grief, it can be challenging to find hope and maintain a positive outlook. However, as we navigate the road to healing, it is crucial to recognize that life is a precious gift. Embracing life's journey, seeking joy, and finding solace in the support of loved ones can lead us towards a brighter future. While the pain from the loss may never completely fade, it is possible to channel that pain into a force that propels us forward, allowing us to live a life that honors [Name]'s memory.

7.8.3 Encouraging a Positive Outlook and Embracing Life's Journey

As we conclude this eulogy and bid our final farewell to our dear departed [Name], let us remember that although [his/her] physical presence may no longer be with us, [his/her] spirit and the love [he/she] brought into our lives will forever remain. May we find solace in the cherished memories we hold dear, and may [his/her] legacy inspire us to live each day to the fullest, embracing life's journey with open hearts and a positive outlook. As we part ways today, let us carry the light of [Name]'s memory within us, spreading love, kindness, and compassion to all we encounter. May our departed loved one, [Name], rest in eternal peace, knowing [he/she] will forever hold a special place in our hearts.

8. Writing Eulogies for Loved Ones Lost to Fire Related Tragedies

In times of immense loss and tragedy, eulogies serve as a powerful tool for healing, remembrance, and celebration of life. When a devastating house fire or other fire related tragedies claim the lives of loved ones, the profound impact of the loss can be overwhelming. Eulogies provide a space for collective mourning, allowing us to honor and remember the individuals who have left us, while also finding solace in shared memories and stories. This chapter explores the significance of eulogies in the wake of fire tragedy, providing insights on writing and delivering meaningful eulogies, highlighting the importance of community support, and offering guidance on navigating the complex journey of grief and mourning. By embracing the power of eulogies, we can find hope, love, and resilience amidst the darkest of times.

8.1 Introduction: Understanding the Power of Eulogies in the Face of Tragedy

In times of tragedy, eulogies serve as a powerful tool for healing and remembrance. They allow us to honor the lives of those we have lost, celebrate their accomplishments, and find solace in shared memories. While the pain of a devastating house fire may seem insurmountable, eulogies offer a way to navigate the grief and pay tribute to the individuals affected by this heartbreaking incident.

8.2 A Brief Overview of the Incident

In the face of tragedy, it is important to acknowledge the heartbreaking realities. Whether it be a devastating house fire that claimed several lives and left a community in mourning or the details of the incident where flames engulfed a home and took away the safety and security that once existed within its walls. It is in these darkest moments that eulogies can bring a glimmer of light and allow us to remember the lives lost.

8.3 Honoring the Lives Lost: Remembering the Individuals Impacted by the Tragedy

Among the rubble and ashes, it is crucial to remember that each life lost holds immense value. As we mourn the victims of the house fire, let us take a moment to appreciate their unique stories and the impact they had on the lives of those around them. Whether it was a neighbor known for their kind smile or a family member who always offered a listening ear, these individuals were an integral part of our community. Through eulogies, we can ensure their memory lives on.

8.4 Crafting Meaningful Eulogies: Tips and Guidelines for Writing and Delivering Eulogies

Crafting a eulogy is a delicate task that requires both compassion and thoughtfulness. Eulogies serve as a way to encapsulate the essence of a person's life, their impact on others, and the legacy they leave behind. To ensure a eulogy captures the true spirit of the individual being honored, it is important to approach the task with sincerity and personal anecdotes. Additionally, remembering to speak from the heart and maintain a sense of grace and poise during the delivery can help create a meaningful tribute to those we have lost.

As we navigate the pain and grief caused by fire tragedy, let us not overlook the power of eulogies to provide solace, preserve memories, and pay homage to those who are no longer with us. In embracing the significance and craft of eulogies, we can find comfort in the shared celebration of lives well-lived and leave a lasting legacy for those lost in the tragedy.

8.5 Sharing Personal Memories and Stories: The Role of Eulogies in Celebrating Lives

8.5.1 How Personal Stories and Memories Contribute to the Eulogy

Eulogies are a chance to celebrate the lives of those we have lost and to honor their memory. One of the most powerful ways to do this is by sharing personal memories and stories. These anecdotes offer a glimpse into the unique qualities and experiences that made the departed special. Whether it's a hilarious childhood mishap that still brings a smile to our faces or a touching act of kindness that touched our hearts, these stories help us remember and cherish the essence of the person we have lost.

8.5.2 Highlighting the Unique Qualities and Achievements of the Deceased

In the eulogy, it's important to showcase the unique qualities and achievements of the deceased. This is a time to celebrate their accomplishments, big or small, and to recognize the impact they had on others. Whether it was their unwavering determination, infectious enthusiasm, or the way they effortlessly made everyone feel loved and heard, these qualities deserve to be celebrated. By highlighting these aspects, we can ensure that their legacy lives on and that their memory continues to inspire and uplift us.

8.6 Healing through Community: The Importance of Coming Together to Support and Mourn

8.6.1 The significance of Community Support in Times of Tragedy

In times of tragedy, the importance of community support cannot be overstated. When a house fire takes away the lives of loved ones, it leaves a void that seems impossible to fill. However, through the support of our community, we can find solace, strength, and a shoulder to lean on. Knowing that we are not alone in our grief, that others are there to offer a listening ear or a comforting hug, can make a world of difference in our healing process.

8.6.2 Creating Spaces for Collective Mourning and Healing

Creating spaces for collective mourning and healing is crucial after such a devastating loss. Whether it's through memorial services, candlelight vigils, or online support groups, providing opportunities for people to come together and share their grief creates a sense of unity and solidarity. These spaces allow individuals to express their emotions, find solace in shared experiences, and begin the healing journey together. Through collective mourning, we find strength in numbers and remind ourselves that even in the darkest times, we have each other.

8.7 Holding Space for Grief: Navigating the Emotional Journey of Loss and Mourning

8.7.1 Understanding the Stages of Grief and Mourning

The emotional journey of loss and mourning is not linear. It's a rollercoaster ride filled with ups and downs, twists and turns. Understanding the stages of grief, from shock and denial to acceptance and finding meaning, can help us navigate this tumultuous journey. It's important to give ourselves permission to feel whatever emotions arise, without judgment or expectation. By acknowledging and honoring our grief, we can gradually move towards healing and finding a new normal.

8.7.2 Resources and Strategies for Coping with Grief

Coping with grief can be overwhelming, and it's important to arm ourselves with resources and strategies to help us through the process. Whether it's seeking professional counseling, joining support groups, or finding solace in creative outlets like writing or painting, discovering what works for us individually can make a significant difference. Although grief may never completely go away, learning healthy ways to cope and finding support along the way can bring a sense of comfort and resilience.

8.8 Moving Forward with Resilience: Finding Hope in the Midst of Tragedy

8.8.1 Finding Strength and Resilience in the Face of Loss

While it may seem impossible to find strength after such a tragic loss, we are often surprised by the resilience that emerges from within. Even in the face of unimaginable grief, we find a determination to honor the memory of our loved ones and live our lives with purpose. Drawing upon the love we shared with them and the lessons they bestowed upon us, we find the inner strength to move forward, one step at a time. Love becomes our guiding light, and resilience becomes our armor.

8.8.2 Embracing Hope and Rebuilding After the Tragedy

In the aftermath of tragedy, it may feel as though hope is a distant and elusive concept. However, it's important to remember that hope can be found even in the darkest of times. As we begin to heal and rebuild, we find hope in the support of our community, the love of our family and friends, and the memories we hold dear. We embrace hope by cherishing the moments we have, by striving to make a positive impact in the world, and by honoring the lives of those we have lost. Together, we can rebuild and create a future filled with love, compassion, and resilience.

As we conclude this exploration into the power of eulogies for those lost to fire related tragedies, know that these heartfelt tributes play a vital role in the healing process. In the act of remembering and celebrating the lives of those we have lost, eulogies provide comfort, support, and community. They remind us that even in the face of tragedy, love and resilience can prevail. May the memories shared and the lessons learned from eulogies continue to inspire us to cherish our loved ones, hold space for grief, and find hope in the midst of adversity.

9. Eulogy 2 - Reflecting on the Bright Spirit of My Grandfather Lost in a Tragic House Fire

9.1 Remembering the Bright Spirit of My Grandfather

9.1.1 Introduction and Greeting

Losing a loved one is never easy, especially when it happens unexpectedly and tragically. The memories of that fateful night when my grandfather, [Name], was taken from us in a devastating house fire will forever be etched in my mind. However, amidst the heart-wrenching grief and devastation, I find solace in reflecting on the bright spirit and remarkable impact he had on my life. I am [Your Name], [Name]'s [Your relationship to the deceased] and I am honored to speak on behalf of the loved ones gathered here to pay tribute. In this eulogy, I will journey through the memories of our time together, explore the profound impact of his loss, and share the valuable lessons learned as we honor his legacy. Join me as we celebrate the life of my grandfather and find inspiration in the enduring love and lessons he left behind.

9.1.2 The Loved Ones who Continue His Legacy

The passing of our dear [Name] has created a significant void in our lives. As we take a moment to contemplate his life, it becomes crucial to recognize those individuals who he held dear. [Name] is survived by [State and name the close kins e.g. his loving family, including his devoted wife [Name] and their [number] children [List Names], who were the center of his universe.] [State and name other relatives e.g. He leaves behind a host of cherished relatives, including, grandchildren, nieces, nephews, and cousins whom he held dear.] Additionally, he touched the lives of countless friends and acquaintances through his graciousness and unwavering support. His presence will be greatly missed by all who had the privilege of knowing him. Although this loss brings immeasurable grief, we find solace in knowing that [Name] has engendered a lasting impact on those whose lives he gracefully enhanced with love and joy.

9.2 A Tragic Night: The House Fire that Changed Everything

9.2.1 The Fateful Evening: Unforeseen Events Unfold

Tip: You may want to recount briefly the event that caused the loss of life. Remember those that provided help during or after the event. For example, you may mention neighbors, passer's by, firefighters who may have tried to assist in putting out the fire or attempting rescue of your loved one.

It was just an ordinary evening when tragedy struck. Little did we know that the very foundation of our lives was about to be shattered. As darkness settled over the neighborhood, a flickering light caught our attention. Flames danced wickedly, their orange glow consuming the sanctuary that was once our home. Panic and fear took hold as we realized the magnitude of the situation. Our lives would never be the same again.

9.2.2 Desperate Moments: Battling the Blaze and Loss

In the chaos that ensued, we fought desperately to save not only our home but also our treasured memories. Firefighters arrived swiftly, their valiant efforts battling the relentless blaze. Yet, despite their heroism, the flames proved relentless, devouring everything in their path. Amidst the chaos, the loss of my grandfather became painfully real. The gravity of the situation began to sink in, leaving us in a state of shock and disbelief.

9.3 The Impact of Loss: Coping with Grief and Devastation

9.3.1 Overwhelming Sadness: Navigating the Initial Shock

In the days following the fire, an overwhelming sadness descended upon our family. The void left by my grandfather's absence was suffocating, and grief consumed our every thought. Each moment was a painful reminder of what we had lost, and the weight of it all felt unbearable. The world seemed to pause, as if mourning alongside us, and we struggled to navigate the unfamiliar terrain of loss.

9.3.2 Emotional Turmoil: Dealing with the Fallout

As time passed, we realized that grief comes in waves, crashing upon us when least expected. The emotional turmoil was both relentless and unpredictable. From the anger and frustration of losing everything, to the profound sadness that lingered, we found ourselves in a constant state of flux. But amidst the chaos, we clung to the memories of my grandfather, drawing strength from the love he had bestowed upon us.

9.4 Cherished Memories: Recalling the Joyful Moments with My Grandfather

9.4.1 Treasured Times: Heartwarming Stories and Laughter

While the pain of his loss is immeasurable, it is the cherished memories of my grandfather that bring light to the darkest of days. From his playful antics and mischievous sense of humor to the heartfelt stories that would leave us in stitches, his presence brought joy and laughter into our lives. Those treasured times spent with him serve as a reminder of the happiness that once filled our home.

9.4.2 Lessons Learned: The Wisdom and Guidance Provided

[**Prompt:** Include a short story or memory of your loved one.]

Beyond the laughter and pranks, my grandfather was a wellspring of wisdom and guidance. He taught us the importance of kindness, resilience, and embracing life's simple pleasures. His words of wisdom resonated deeply within us, becoming guiding lights during times of darkness. As we continue to navigate the aftermath of his loss, we find solace in living by the principles he instilled in us.

While the pain of losing my grandfather in such a tragic way will never fully dissipate, I choose to honor his memory by celebrating the bright spirit that continues to live on within me. In the midst of grief and devastation, I hold onto the joyful moments and valuable lessons he left behind, for they are a testament to the enduring impact he had on my life.

9.5 Lessons Learned: Finding Strength and Resilience in the Face of Tragedy

9.5.1 Embracing Resilience: The Power of the Human Spirit

In the wake of a devastating tragedy, we often discover a wellspring of strength within ourselves that we never knew existed. The human spirit has an incredible capacity for resilience, allowing us to face unimaginable pain and loss with determination and grace. Despite the heartache of losing my beloved grandfather in a tragic house fire, I have come to realize that we are capable of finding light even in the darkest of times. This experience has taught me the power of resilience and the indomitable spirit that resides within each and every one of us.

9.5.2 Coping Mechanisms: Discovering Ways to Heal and Grow

When faced with the shattering reality of losing someone dear, it's important to find healthy ways to cope and navigate the difficult emotions that arise. Each person's journey is unique, and finding the right coping mechanisms is crucial to the healing process. For me, writing about my feelings and connecting with others who have experienced similar losses has been a tremendous source of comfort. Engaging in activities that bring solace, such as meditation, art, or spending time in nature, can be invaluable tools for healing and personal growth. It is through these coping mechanisms that we can begin to find hope and strength amidst the pain.

9.6 Honoring His Legacy: Keeping the Spirit of My Grandfather Alive

9.6.1 Celebrating a Life: Commemorating his Impact and Values

Though my grandfather may no longer be with us physically, his impact on our lives continues to shine brightly. Honoring his legacy means celebrating the incredible person he was and carrying forward the values he held dear. Commemorating his life through storytelling, sharing cherished memories, and keeping his spirit alive in our hearts allows us to feel connected to him in a meaningful way. By embracing his love, kindness, and wisdom, we ensure that his presence remains a guiding force in our lives.

9.6.2 Continuing Traditions: Carrying Forward his Love and Passions

One of the most beautiful ways to honor someone we have lost is by continuing the traditions they held dear. My grandfather had a deep love for family gatherings, where laughter and good food were always abundant. By keeping these traditions alive, we not only pay tribute to his memory but also keep the bond between generations strong. In pursuing his passions, whether it be gardening, fishing, or storytelling, we carry forward the love and joy he brought into our lives. In these acts, we find comfort and a sense of kinship that keeps his spirit alive.

9.7 Finding Closure: Navigating the Healing Process and Moving Forward

9.7.1 Seeking Closure: Embracing Healing and Acceptance

Finding closure after a tragic loss is a deeply personal journey, and there is no one-size-fits-all solution. It is essential to give ourselves permission to grieve, allowing the waves of sorrow to wash over us. In time, acceptance begins to take hold, and we can start to heal. Through therapy, support groups, or simply confiding in loved ones, we can find solace and understanding. Closure comes when we acknowledge the pain, honor our emotions, and gradually open ourselves to the possibility of moving forward while keeping our loved one close to our hearts.

9.7.2 Supporting Each Other: Finding Strength in Family and Loved Ones

During times of loss, our loved ones become our pillars of support, offering a shoulder to lean on and a listening ear. Coming together as a family, we find solace and strength in one another. Sharing our grief, memories, and stories not only helps us heal but also strengthens the bonds that hold us together. In supporting each other through the grieving process, we create a network of love and understanding that becomes a source of comfort during the most challenging times.

9.8 The Bright Spirit Lives On: Embracing the Lessons and Love Shared

9.8.1 Carrying his Legacy: How his Spirit Continues to Inspire

While the physical presence of our loved ones may fade, the impact they have on our lives remains everlasting. By embracing the lessons and love we shared with our late grandfather, we can walk forward with his spirit as our guiding light. His wisdom, resilience, and zest for life continue to inspire us as we navigate our own journeys. Through his influence, we learn to cherish every moment, find strength in adversity, and spread kindness to all those we encounter.

9.8.2 Lessons for Life: Applying the Wisdom Gained from his Presence

The wisdom imparted by our loved ones stays with us long after they are gone. From my grandfather, I learned the importance of laughter, the value of hard work, and the significance of finding joy in the simple moments of life. Applying these lessons to my own life has allowed me to navigate challenges with a newfound resilience and an appreciation for the beauty that surrounds me. By carrying forward his teachings, we ensure that the impact of his life extends far beyond his physical presence, shaping our own paths and the lives of those around us.

As I conclude this reflection on the bright spirit of my grandfather, [Name] lost in that tragic house fire, I am reminded that his love, wisdom, and legacy will forever live on within us. While the pain of his loss will never fully fade, we can find comfort in the cherished memories we shared and the lessons we have learned. Through resilience and a commitment to honor his memory, we can move forward, carrying his spirit with us every step of the way. May his bright spirit continue to guide and inspire us, reminding us of the power of love, resilience, and the enduring impact of a life well-lived.

10. Lessons from Tragedy: Sharing Memories of Someone Who Succumbed to Drugs

10.1 Introduction: The Power of Eulogies in Honoring Lives Lost to Drugs

Eulogies serve as a profound way to remember and pay tribute to those who have tragically succumbed to the ravages of drug addiction. Each individual's story is unique, and through the art of eulogizing, we can celebrate their lives, commemorate their accomplishments, and reflect upon the challenges they faced. This chapter explores the significance of sharing memories through eulogies for those lost to drugs. It delves into understanding the causes and impact of drug addiction, while emphasizing the importance of destigmatizing the issue. Furthermore, we delve into strategies for prevention and recovery, as well as the power of eulogies in inspiring change and advocacy. By shining a light on these personal narratives, we can foster compassion, empathy, and hope in the face of this ongoing crisis.

10.2 Understanding the Tragedy: Exploring the Causes and Impact of Drug Addiction

10.2.1 The Rise of Drug Addiction: A Growing Crisis

The rise of drug addiction is a sobering reality that we cannot ignore. It has become a crisis affecting people from all walks of life, regardless of age, gender, or background. Understanding the factors contributing to this epidemic is crucial in addressing the issue head-on. By recognizing the social, economic, and psychological factors that push individuals towards substance abuse, we can work towards prevention and support.

10.2.2 The Impact on Individuals, Families, and Communities

Drug addiction has far-reaching consequences that extend beyond the individual struggling with substance abuse. It affects families, friends, and entire communities. The pain, heartbreak, and devastation caused by drugs are immeasurable. Exploring the impact addiction has on those left behind helps us understand the urgency with which we must address this crisis and offer support, compassion, and resources to those affected.

10.3 Remembering the Individual: Celebrating the Life and Personality of the Deceased

10.3.1 Anecdotes and Stories that Capture the Deceased's Spirit

When delivering a eulogy for someone who succumbed to drugs, it is important to remember them for the person they were beyond their struggles. Sharing anecdotes and stories that capture their spirit allows us to celebrate their unique personality, quirks, and passions. By focusing on the joy they brought into our lives, we can ensure their memory lives on and is not defined solely by their addiction.

10.3.2 Highlighting Achievements and Contributions

Every person, regardless of their struggle, has achievements and contributions worth celebrating. Acknowledging the accomplishments and positive impact the deceased had on others helps us recognize the significance of their existence. By highlighting their kindness, talents, and accomplishments, we remind ourselves that drug addiction does not define a person, but rather, it was one part of their complex journey.

10.4 Lessons Learned: Addressing the Stigma and Misconceptions Surrounding Drug Addiction

10.4.1 Challenging Preconceived Notions about Addiction

One of the lessons we can learn from tragedy is to challenge the preconceived notions and stereotypes surrounding drug addiction. It is easy to villainize or judge those who struggle, but through sharing our experiences and stories, we can promote empathy, understanding, and compassion. By addressing the stigma associated with addiction, we create a safer space for open dialogue and pave the way for effective solutions.

10.4.2 Dispelling Myths: Understanding the Complexity of Addiction

Addiction is a complex issue that cannot be reduced to simple explanations or judgments. Disentangling the myths and misconceptions surrounding drug addiction is essential in fostering a more informed society. By educating ourselves and others about the biological, psychological, and environmental factors that contribute to addiction, we can better support those in need and advocate for change in policies and treatments.

10.5 Conclusion: Honoring Lives Lost to Drugs

In conclusion, eulogies serve as a powerful tool in remembering and honoring lives lost to drugs. By celebrating the individual beyond their struggles, understanding the causes and impact of drug addiction, and addressing the stigma and misconceptions about this issue, we can contribute to a more compassionate and supportive society. In sharing memories and lessons, we can find solace, honor the deceased, and inspire change.

11. Eulogy 3 - Remembering our Loved One Lost to Drug Overdose

11.1 Introduction: Honoring the Life of our Loved One and Shedding Light on Drug Overdose

11.1.1 Setting the Stage: The Importance of Remembering and Honoring

Drug overdose is a devastating reality that claims far too many lives, leaving behind grief-stricken families and communities struggling to make sense of the loss. In this heartfelt tribute, we gather to remember and celebrate the life of [Name], who was taken from us too soon due to a drug overdose. I am [Your Name], [Name]'s [Your relationship to the deceased] and I am honored to speak on behalf of the loved ones gathered here today to pay tribute. Today we aim to honor [his/her] memory, highlighting [his/her] achievements, impact, and the light they brought into the world. It also seeks to shed light on the dark and difficult challenges faced by those battling addiction and the stigma surrounding it. As we share stories, reflect on lessons learned, and advocate for change, we hope to encourage open dialogue, support, and prevention efforts to prevent further tragedies. Let us come together to remember [Name] and ensure [his/her] light continues to shine brightly in the fight against drug overdose.

11.1.2 The Loved Ones who Continue the Legacy

The departure of our dearly departed [Name] has inflicted a deep and profound void within the depths of our souls. As we take a moment to contemplate upon [his/her] life, it becomes absolutely crucial to recognize the esteemed individuals who held an irreplaceable place within [his/her] heart. [Name] is survived by [State and name the close kins e.g. [his/her] loving family, including [his/her] devoted [husband/wife] [Name] and their [number] children [List Names], who were the center of [his/her] universe.] [State and name other relatives e.g. [He/She] leaves behind a host of cherished relatives, including nieces, nephews, and cousins whom [he/she] held dear.] Additionally, [he/she] touched the lives of countless friends and acquaintances through [his/her] graciousness and unwavering support. [His/Her] presence will be greatly missed by all who had the privilege of knowing [him/her]. Although this loss brings immeasurable grief, we find solace in knowing that [Name] has engendered a lasting impact on those whose lives [he/she] gracefully enhanced with love and joy.

11.2 Celebrating [Name]'s Life: Fond Memories, Achievements, and Impact

As we gather to celebrate the beautiful life of [Name], let's reflect on the cherished memories we shared with [him/her], the laughter, the love, and the moments that brought us closer. [Name] had a way of lighting up a room, and [his/her] infectious energy will forever be etched in our hearts.

Beyond the joy [he/she] gave us, [Name] achieved great things in [his/her] too-short time. Whether it was [his/her] career accomplishments, creative endeavors, or personal milestones, [he/she] made [his/her] mark on the world and left behind a legacy worth celebrating.

But perhaps what truly defines a person's life is the impact they had on others. [Name] touched the lives of those around [him/her], leaving imprints of kindness, compassion, and love. Through [his/her] generosity and genuine care, [he/she] made our lives richer and inspired us to be better versions of ourselves. Let's remember the ways in which [Name] made a difference, no matter how small, and carry that light forward.

[**Prompt:** Share 1 or 2 memories or stories of your loved one's impact on others or yourself here.]

11.3 The Darkness of Drug Overdose: Understanding the Challenges Faced

As we gather to remember [Name], it is crucial to acknowledge the complex and challenging circumstances that led to [his/her] tragic loss. Drug overdose is a harsh reality that affects countless individuals and their families every day. It is a struggle that often goes unseen, but it is important to shed light on it to raise awareness and promote understanding.

There are various factors contributing to drug overdose, including societal pressures, mental health issues, and the grip of addiction. Understanding these challenges can help us come together to support those who are still fighting, while also providing solace to families grappling with the aftermath of losing a loved one.

The toll on families is immeasurable. The emotional and psychological impact can be overwhelming, leaving loved ones grappling with guilt, grief, and a myriad of emotions. It is essential for us to extend our compassion and support to the families affected by drug overdose, as they navigate their way through this difficult journey.

11.4 The Power of Love and Support: Family and Friends Coming Together

In the face of such darkness, love and support become beacons of hope. When we come together as a community, as friends and family, we can provide the strength needed to weather the storm. Support networks play a vital role in helping individuals find solace, understanding, and guidance during these difficult times.

Families and friends have an incredible capacity to offer support to one another. By lending an ear, extending a helping hand, or simply being present, we can provide comfort and companionship to those who need it most. Together, we can navigate the painful journey of grief and begin to heal.

Group therapy and supportive communities also offer a safe space for healing. Sharing experiences, stories, and emotions with others who have walked similar paths can provide a sense of belonging and understanding. Through these connections, we find the courage to carry on and honor the memory of [Name].

11.5 Conclusion: A Light that Continues to Shine

Let us hold onto the memories of [Name], celebrating the light [he/she] brought into our lives. May we also remember the importance of supporting one another through the darkness, and work towards a world where no more lives are tragically lost to drug overdose. Let [Name]'s light guide us towards a brighter future.

As we conclude this heartfelt eulogy for [Name], let us carry [his/her] light with us as a source of inspiration and motivation. May [his/her] memory serve as a reminder of the importance of love, support, and understanding in battling addiction and preventing drug overdose. Let us continue to break the silence, share our stories, and support one another in this ongoing journey. Together, we can honor [Name] and countless others lost, ensuring their legacies live on to create a brighter, safer future for all.

12. Eulogy 4 - Honoring the Life of a Tragic Drowning Victim

12.1 Introduction: Remembering the Life of Our Loved One

12.1.1 Addressing this Great Loss

The passing of a loved one is always a deeply painful and challenging experience. In the case of [Name], [his/her] life was tragically cut short due to a drowning accident. However, amidst the sorrow and heartache, it is crucial to honor and celebrate the beautiful life [he/she] lived. I am [Your Name], [Name]'s [your relationship to the deceased] and I am honored to speak on behalf of the loved ones gathered here today to pay tribute. This eulogy serves as a heartfelt tribute to [Name], a cherished individual who touched the lives of many. Through exploring [his/her] early life, accomplishments, cherished memories, and the lessons we can learn from [his/her] untimely passing, we aim to keep [his/her] spirit alive and inspire others to embrace life and advocate for water safety.

12.1.2 The Purpose of the Eulogy

Ladies and gentlemen, as we gather here today to honor the life of our beloved [Name], it is with heavy hearts but also with gratitude for the time we were fortunate enough to spend with [him/her]. The purpose of this eulogy is not to dwell on the tragic circumstances that took [Name] away from us, but rather to celebrate the beautiful life [he/she] lived and the impact [he/she] had on each of us. Today, let us come together to share stories, remember cherished moments, and find solace in the knowledge that [Name] will forever hold a special place in our hearts.

12.1.3 The Loved Ones who Continue the Legacy

Our beloved [Name]'s passing has left a profound void in our lives. In reflecting on [his/her] life, it is important to acknowledge those who continue to carry on [his/her] legacy. [Name] is survived by [State and name the close kins e.g. [his/her] loving family, including [his/her] devoted [husband/wife] [Name] and their [number] children [List Names], who were the center of [his/her] universe.] [State and name other relatives e.g. [He/She] leaves behind a host of cherished relatives, including nieces, nephews, and cousins whom [he/she] held dear.] Additionally, [he/she] touched the lives of countless friends and acquaintances through [his/her] graciousness and unwavering support. [His/Her] presence will be greatly missed by all who had the privilege of knowing [him/her]. Although this loss brings immeasurable grief, we find solace in knowing that [Name] has left a lasting impact on those whose lives [he/she] gracefully enhanced with love and joy.

12.2 Early Life and Influences: A Journey of Joy and Inspiration

12.2.1 Childhood Memories and Family Bond

In the early years of [Name]'s life, it was clear that [he/she] was destined for greatness. From [his/her] infectious laughter to [his/her] curious spirit, [Name] brought joy to everyone [he/she] encountered. Growing up with [his/her] loving family, [he/she] developed a bond that remained unbreakable throughout [his/her] life. [His/Her] childhood was filled with countless memories of laughter, love, and the unwavering support of [his/her] family.

12.2.2 Educational Journey and Academic Achievements

[Name]'s passion for learning and thirst for knowledge led [him/her] on a remarkable educational journey. [His/Her] dedication and hard work in school resulted in numerous academic achievements. From receiving top honors to excelling in [his/her] chosen field, [Name] never settled for mediocrity. [He/She] pushed boundaries, embraced challenges, and proved time and again that with determination, anything was possible.

12.2.3 Passion and Hobbies: Our Beloved's Unique Talents

Tip: *It is important to remember the deceased's likes, quirks and talents.*

[**Prompt:** Share in a short story some of the likes, quirks and unique talents of the deceased.]

Beyond [his/her] academic pursuits, [Name] had a multitude of passions and hobbies that added vibrancy to [his/her] life. Whether it was painting breathtaking landscapes, strumming [his/her] guitar, or writing poetry that stirred the soul, [Name] possessed a unique talent for creativity. [His/Her] talents not only brought [him/her] joy but also touched the lives of those fortunate enough to witness [his/her] expressions of art.

12.3 Passion and Achievements: Celebrating Accomplishments

12.3.1 Professional Achievements and Career Milestones

In [his/her] professional life, [Name] achieved great success and left an indelible mark on [his/her] chosen career path. Through determination and unwavering commitment, [he/she] climbed the ladder of success, accomplishing milestones that inspired others. [Name] not only excelled in [his/her] own endeavors but also selflessly supported and uplifted those around [him/her], believing in the power of collaboration and collective growth.

12.3.2 Contributions to the Community and Philanthropy

[Name]'s impact extended far beyond [his/her] professional achievements. [He/She] understood the importance of giving back to the community and dedicated [himself/herself] to making a positive difference in the lives of others. Whether it was volunteering at local shelters, organizing fundraisers for important causes, or lending a helping hand to those in need, [Name] was a beacon of compassion and empathy. [His/Her] selflessness will forever serve as an inspiration to us all.

12.3.3 Personal Growth and Overcoming Challenges

Along [his/her] journey, [Name] faced [his/her] fair share of challenges. Yet, [he/she] approached each obstacle with unwavering determination and an optimism that was contagious. Through personal growth and self-reflection, [Name] not only overcame [his/her] own hurdles but also became a source of strength for others facing similar struggles. [His/Her] resilience and unwavering spirit remind us that even in the darkest times, there is always a glimmer of hope.

12.4 Precious Memories: Cherished Moments Shared with Our Beloved

12.4.1 Family Gatherings and Traditions

Some of the fondest memories of [Name] are those shared during family gatherings and cherished traditions. From holiday celebrations filled with laughter and delicious food to annual reunions that brought loved ones from near and far, [Name] was the glue that held the family together. [His/Her] infectious spirit and love for family made every moment spent together a treasured memory.

12.4.2 Friendships and Shared Adventures

Beyond [his/her] extraordinary relationships with family, [Name] had an uncanny ability to form deep and lasting friendships. [His/Her] genuine care, infectious humor, and willingness to always be there for [his/her] friends created an unbreakable bond. Together, they embarked on countless adventures, from road trips to spontaneous escapades, leaving behind a trail of laughter and unforgettable memories.

12.4.3 Impact on the Lives of Loved Ones

It is impossible to quantify the impact [Name] had on the lives of those around [him/her]. [His/Her] kindness, compassion, and unwavering support touched the hearts of all who had the privilege of knowing [him/her]. [Name] had a unique ability to lift spirits, inspire others to pursue their dreams, and remind us all of the beauty of life. [His/Her] memory will forever live on in the lives [he/she] touched, and [his/her] legacy will continue to inspire generations to come.

Today, as we bid farewell to [Name], let us not dwell on the tragedy that took [him/her] away from us, but rather focus on the gift [he/she] was in our lives. Let us honor [his/her] memory by living each day with the same passion, kindness, and zest for life that defined [Name]. May [his/her] spirit guide us through the stormy times and serve as a reminder of the preciousness of every moment we are blessed with. [Name], you will be deeply missed, but never forgotten.

12.5 The Tragic Incident: Reflecting on the Drowning Accident

12.5.1 The Circumstances Surrounding the Accident

In a blink of an eye, our lives were forever changed. [Name] was taken from us in a tragic drowning accident. It is difficult to comprehend how such a devastating incident could occur, but we must remember that life is full of uncertainties. We gather here today to reflect on the circumstances surrounding this heartbreaking incident, and to find solace in each other's presence.

12.5.2 Coping with the Initial Shock and Grief

When we received the news, it felt like the world had shattered into a million pieces. The shock was overwhelming, and the grief that followed was indescribable. We each coped in our own ways – some turned to tears, others to silence. But through it all, we found strength in knowing that we were not alone in our pain. We leaned on each other and came together as a family, supporting one another through the darkest of days.

12.5.3 Finding Strength in Unity and Support

In the midst of this tragedy, we experienced an outpouring of love and support from friends, neighbors, and even strangers. It reminded us that even in the face of darkness, there is still goodness in this world. We were humbled by the acts of kindness and generosity that helped us carry the weight of our grief. At times like these, it is the unity and support that emerges from the darkness that gives us the strength to move forward.

12.6 Lessons Learned: Advocating for Water Safety and Awareness

12.6.1 Promoting Water Safety Measures

As we come to terms with this devastating loss, we feel a deep sense of responsibility to prevent such tragedies from happening to others. We vow to become advocates for water safety measures, spreading awareness and encouraging proper precautions to save lives. May [Name]'s accident serve as a wake-up call to us all to prioritize safety when enjoying the water.

12.6.2 Educating Others on Drowning Prevention

Education is key in preventing future drownings. We must ensure that everyone, from children to adults, understands the importance of water safety. By providing resources, information, and swimming lessons, we can equip individuals with the knowledge to make safe choices in and around bodies of water. Let us honor [Name]'s memory by taking proactive steps to prevent such tragedies in the future.

12.6.3 Supporting Organizations and Initiatives

In our efforts to raise awareness and prevent future drownings, we will support organizations and initiatives dedicated to water safety. By joining forces with like-minded individuals and communities, we can amplify our impact and create a safer environment for everyone. Together, we can turn our grief into a catalyst for change.

12.7 Love and Support: Coming Together in Grief and Strength

12.7.1 The Power of Family and Community Support

In times of immense sorrow, the power of love and support is immeasurable. We are incredibly grateful for the unwavering love and support of our family and community during this trying time. The compassion and empathy that has poured into our lives has been a source of comfort and strength. It reminds us that even in our darkest moments, we are not alone.

12.7.2 Honoring Our Beloved Through Shared Memories

As we gather today, let us take a moment to cherish the memories we shared with [Name]. [His/Her] laughter, kindness, and zest for life will forever be etched in our hearts. Through these shared memories, we keep [Name] alive in our thoughts and ensure that [his/her] spirit lives on.

12.7.3 Coping Mechanisms and Healing Together

Grief is a journey unique to each individual, but we can find solace in walking this path together. Let us lean on one another for support, understanding that in our collective sorrow, there is strength. Whether it's through sharing stories, seeking professional help, or simply being present for one another, we will navigate this painful journey side by side, helping each other heal and find moments of peace.

12.8 Remembering A Life That Continues to Inspire

12.8.1 Remembering Our Loved One's Impact on Others

Although [Name] may no longer be physically with us, [his/her] impact on our lives continues to resonate. [He/She] touched the lives of many, leaving behind a legacy of love, kindness, and compassion. Each of us carries a piece of [Name] within us, and it is through our actions and the way we live our lives that we honor [his/her] memory.

12.8.2 Continuing Our Beloved's Passions and Dreams

In remembrance of [Name], let us strive to carry forward [his/her] passions and dreams. Whether it's pursuing a career in [his/her] field of interest, supporting causes [he/she] believed in, or simply embodying [his/her] zest for life, we can keep [Name]'s spirit alive by embracing the things that brought [him/her] joy.

12.8.3 Cherishing Memories and Keeping Our Loved One's Spirit Alive

As time passes, it is important for us to continue cherishing [Name]'s memory. Whether it's through creating a memorial, sharing stories, or keeping [his/her] favorite traditions alive, we can ensure that [his/her] spirit remains a vibrant part of our lives. [Name] may be gone, but [his/her] light will forever shine in our hearts. In closing, as we bid farewell to [Name], let us remember the joy, love, and inspiration [he/she] brought into our lives. Though [his/her] absence will be deeply felt, [his/her] legacy will continue to shine brightly. May we honor [his/her] memory by embracing [his/her] passions, supporting water safety initiatives, and cherishing the precious moments we have with our loved ones. Let [Name]'s life be a constant reminder to live fully, love deeply, and never take a single day for granted. [He/She] may be gone, but [his/her] spirit will forever remain in our hearts. Rest in peace, dear [Name].

13. Eulogy 5 - A Tender Eulogy for a Loved One Lost to an Accidental Fall

13.1 Introduction: For a Loved One Lost to an Accidental Fall

13.1.1 Remembering the Life and Legacy of Our Loved One

Losing a loved one in a tragic accident, such as an accidental fall, can be an incredibly difficult and painful experience. Today we take a moment to reflect on the life and legacy of [Name], who was taken from us too soon. I am [Your Name], [Name]'s [Your relationship to the deceased] and I am honored to speak on behalf of the loved ones gathered here today. As we navigate the depths of grief, it becomes essential to honor the memory of our loved one by cherishing [his/her] achievements and contributions. We delve into the circumstances surrounding the fatal fall, seeking understanding and closure. Together, we embrace [Name]'s lasting legacy and discover ways to move forward with love and resilience.

13.1.2 The Importance of Reflecting on Our Beloved's Legacy

Losing a loved one is never easy, and when it happens due to an unexpected accident, the shock and grief can be even more overwhelming. In times like these, it becomes crucial for us to reflect on the life and legacy of the departed. [Name] may no longer physically be with us, but [his/her] impact and memories live on, shaping and influencing our lives in countless ways. By taking the time to honor and remember [his/her] legacy, we can find solace and meaning amidst the heartache.

13.1.3 The Loved Ones who Continue the Legacy

Our beloved [Name]'s passing has left a profound void in our lives. In reflecting on [his/her] life, it is important to acknowledge those who continue to carry on [his/her] legacy. [Name] is survived by [State and name the close kins e.g. [his/her] loving family, including [his/her] devoted [husband/wife] [Name] and their [number] children [List Names], who were the center of [his/her] universe.] [State and name other relatives e.g. [He/She] leaves behind a host of cherished relatives, including nieces, nephews, and cousins whom [he/she] held dear.] Additionally, [he/she] touched the lives of countless friends and acquaintances through [his/her] graciousness and unwavering support. [His/Her] presence will be greatly missed by all who had the privilege of knowing [him/her]. Although this loss brings immeasurable grief, we find solace in knowing that [Name] has engendered a lasting impact on those whose lives [he/she] gracefully enhanced with love and joy.

13.2 The Tragic Accident: Understanding the Circumstances of the Fatal Fall

13.2.1 Recounting the Details of the Accidental Fall

Tip: It is important to approach this part of the reflection with sensitivity, keeping in mind that accidents can happen to anyone at any time.

The tragic loss of [Name] stemmed from an accidental fall that took place on [date]. Although accidents are often unforeseeable and random, coming to terms with the details surrounding the fall can provide some clarity amidst the confusion.

13.2.2 Investigating Contributing Factors

Tip: While it is difficult to pinpoint exact causes for accidents, it's worth considering any contributing factors that might have played a role in [Name]'s fatal fall. Factors such as environmental conditions, physical impairments, or any other relevant circumstances can offer insight into how the accident occurred. However, it's essential to remember that assigning blame is not the purpose here, but rather to better comprehend the incident and potentially prevent similar tragedies in the future.

13.3 The Impact of Our Beloved's Life: Celebrating the Achievements and Contributions

13.3.1 Highlighting Accomplishments and Milestones

Tip: *One of the most beautiful ways to honor the memory of loved ones is by celebrating their achievements and milestones. Whether it be personal or professional accomplishments, their impact on the lives of others, or any significant goals they achieved, taking the time to highlight these moments allows us to appreciate the fullness of their life and the legacy they left behind.*

[**Prompt:** Share details about personal or professional accomplishments of the dearly departed.]

13.3.2 Recognizing Our Beloved's Contributions to the Community

Tip: Often, our loved ones make valuable contributions to their communities, big or small, that we may not fully recognize or appreciate until they are gone. Sharing and acknowledging the ways in which the deceased positively impacted the lives of others can bring comfort and pride, reminding us of the importance of community and the lasting influence one person can have.

[**Prompt:** Share details acknowledging the ways in which the deceased positively impacted the lives of others and contributed to the community.]

13.4 Grief and Healing: Navigating the Emotional Journey of Loss

13.4.1 Understanding the Stages of Grief

Grief is a complex and personal journey, and there is no right way to navigate it. However, familiarizing ourselves with the stages of grief, such as denial, anger, bargaining, depression, and acceptance, can provide a framework for understanding our emotions and reactions. It's important to remember that everyone experiences grief differently, so allowing ourselves and others the space to process and heal in their own way is paramount.

13.4.2. Coping Strategies for Dealing with Loss

While grief may never fully dissipate, there are coping strategies that can help ease the pain and support the healing process. Seeking support from friends, family, or support groups, engaging in self-care activities, expressing emotions through writing or art, and honoring the memory of [Name] through rituals or acts of remembrance are just a few ways to navigate the challenging path of loss.

In remembering [Name]'s life and legacy, we not only honor [his/her] memory but also find strength, comfort, and inspiration for our own journeys ahead. Let us reflect on [his/her] impact and cherish the time we had together, knowing that [he/she] will forever hold a place in our hearts and lives.

13.5 Conclusion: Embracing Our Beloved's Legacy and Moving Forward with Love and Resilience

In closing, as we pen this tender eulogy for [Name], we remember [his/her] life with gratitude and love. While the pain of [his/her] accidental fall may never fully dissipate, we find solace in celebrating [Name]'s achievements and contributions, and in the stories and memories shared by those whose lives [he/she] touched. Together, we gather strength from our community of support, navigating the journey of grief and healing. As we bid farewell to our beloved [Name], we carry [his/her] legacy in our hearts, embracing the lessons learned and cherishing the time we had. With love and resilience, we face the future, honoring [Name] by living our lives to the fullest. May [his/her] soul rest in eternal peace.

14. Eulogy 6 - A Tribute to the Beautiful Life (Generic)

14.1 Introduction and Greeting

14.1.1 Remembering the Beautiful Life of Our Dearly Departed

It is with heavy hearts and profound sadness that we gather here today to pay tribute to the beautiful life of [Name]. [Name]'s presence in our lives was a gift beyond measure, and [his/her] untimely departure has left an indelible void that can never be filled. I am [Your Name], [Name]'s [Your relationship to the deceased] and I am honored to speak on behalf of the loved ones gathered here. Today, we come together to remember, honor, and celebrate the extraordinary person that [Name] was. Through [his/her] childhood memories, achievements, passions, loving relationships, and the wisdom [he/she] imparted, we will reflect on the impact [Name] had on our lives. As we cope with this profound loss, we find solace in the knowledge that [Name]'s spirit will forever be cherished, and [his/her] legacy will continue to inspire us as we carry [his/her] light forward.

14.1.2 Celebrating a Life Cut Short

We gather here today to remember and honor the beautiful life of [Name], a person who left us far too soon. Though our hearts are heavy with grief, let us also celebrate the joy, love, and impact that [Name] brought into our lives. [His/Her] departure may be a painful reminder of life's unpredictability, but it also serves as a reminder to truly cherish every moment we have with those we hold dear.

14.1.3 The Loved Ones who Continue the Legacy

Our beloved [Name]'s passing has left a profound void in our lives. In reflecting on [his/her] life, it is important to acknowledge those who continue to carry on [his/her] legacy. [Name] is survived by [State and name the close kins e.g. [his/her] loving family, including [his/her] devoted [husband/wife] [Name] and their [number] children [List Names], who were the center of [his/her] universe.] [State and name other relatives e.g. [He/She] leaves behind a host of cherished relatives, including nieces, nephews, and cousins whom [he/she] held dear.] Additionally, [he/she] touched the lives of countless friends and acquaintances through [his/her] graciousness and unwavering support. [His/Her] presence will be greatly missed by all who had the privilege of knowing [him/her]. Although this loss brings immeasurable grief, we find solace in knowing that [Name] has left a lasting impact on those whose lives [he/she] gracefully enhanced with love and joy.

14.2 Childhood Memories: A Glimpse into the Early Years

14.2.1 Early Family Life and Background

In [Name]'s early years, [his/her] family provided a strong foundation for the remarkable person [he/she] would become. Born and raised in [place], [Name] was surrounded by love and support from [his/her] parents and siblings. These formative years played a crucial role in shaping [Name]'s character and values, providing a sense of stability that would accompany [him/her] throughout life.

14.2.2 Memorable Childhood Stories and Adventures

Childhood memories often hold a special place in our hearts, and [Name] was no exception. From adventurous family vacations to silly escapades with friends, [Name] had a knack for infusing joy into every moment. Whether it was building forts in the backyard or initiating impromptu dance parties, [his/her] infectious laughter and zest for life brought happiness to all who knew [him/her].

14.3 Achievements and Passions: Celebrating Accomplishments

14.3.1 Academic and Professional Milestones

[Name] possessed a remarkable drive and determination that propelled [him/her] to achieve great things. Academically, [he/she] soared to new heights, always striving for excellence. [His/Her] accomplishments were not limited to the classroom, as [Name] also excelled in [his/her] professional pursuits, leaving an indelible mark on [his/her] chosen field.

14.3.2 Personal and Creative Achievements

Beyond the realm of academia and work, [Name] pursued [his/her] passions with unwavering enthusiasm. Whether it was painting, writing, playing an instrument, or participating in sports, [Name] embraced [his/her] creative side and used it as a means of self-expression. [His/Her] talents were undeniable, and [his/her] ability to inspire others through [his/her] creativity was truly exceptional.

14.4 Loving Relationships: Cherishing the Impact on Family and Friends

14.4.1 The Love and Support of the Immediate Family

No tribute to [Name] would be complete without acknowledging the love and support they received from [his/her] immediate family. [His/Her] parents, siblings, and extended family members were an unwavering source of encouragement and provided a strong support system throughout [Name]'s journey. Their bond will forever be a testament to the power of familial love.

14.4.2 Lifelong Friends and the Bonds They Shared

In addition to [his/her] family, [Name] cultivated deep and meaningful friendships that lasted a lifetime. These cherished connections brought joy, laughter, and a sense of belonging to [Name]'s life. The impact [he/she] had on [his/her] friends, and the impact [his/her] friends had on [him/her], will continue to resonate in the hearts of all who were fortunate enough to know [Name].

14.4.3 Our Beloved's Impact on the Community and Beyond

[Name]'s influence extended far beyond [his/her] inner circle, as [he/she] also made a significant impact on the community. [His/Her] kindness, compassion, and willingness to lend a helping hand touched the lives of many. Whether through volunteering, advocacy work, or simply being a source of comfort to those in need, [Name] made the world a better place with every action [he/she] took.

As we bid farewell to [Name], let us carry [his/her] memory in our hearts. May we find solace in the love [he/she] shared, the memories we hold dear, and the legacy [he/she] left behind. Though we mourn [his/her] loss, let us also embrace the valuable lessons [he/she] taught us about living passionately, loving wholeheartedly, and making every moment count.

14.5 Lessons Learned: Reflecting on the Wisdom Our Beloved Shared with Us

14.5.1 Words of Wisdom and Life Lessons

In the midst of our grief, let us take a moment to reflect on the valuable lessons and words of wisdom that [Name] shared with us. [Name] had a unique way of imparting knowledge and guidance, often through [his/her] storytelling or simple yet profound statements. Whether it was reminding us to embrace each day with gratitude or encouraging us to always follow our dreams, [Name]'s wisdom resonated deeply with those fortunate enough to have known [him/her].

14.5.2 Influence on Our Personal Growth and Development

The impact [Name] had on our personal growth and development cannot be overstated. [Name] possessed an innate ability to inspire and motivate others to become better versions of themselves. Through [his/her] infectious enthusiasm and unwavering belief in our potential, [Name] pushed us to step out of our comfort zones and embrace new challenges. [His/Her] encouragement and support were instrumental in helping us discover our own strengths and achieve personal milestones we once thought were beyond our reach.

14.6 Honoring Our Loved One's Spirit and Zest for Life

14.6.1 Embracing Our Beloved's Sense of Adventure and Curiosity

Let us honor and celebrate [Name]'s spirit, which was filled to the brim with a sense of adventure and curiosity. [Name] had an insatiable hunger for new experiences and a contagious zest for life. [He/She] infused every moment with excitement and taught us the beauty of embracing the unknown. In [his/her] honor, let's take a cue from [Name] and embark on our own daring escapades, savoring each moment with the same enthusiasm that [he/she] did.

14.6.2 OurLoved One's Passion for Making a Difference

Another remarkable characteristic that defined [Name] was [his/her] unwavering passion for making a difference in the world. [Name] understood the power of compassion and believed in the ability of a single individual to create positive change. Whether it was volunteering at local shelters or tirelessly advocating for causes close to [his/her] heart, [Name] showed us that even the smallest actions can have a profound impact. Let us carry forward [Name]'s legacy by following in [his/her] footsteps and continuing [his/her] noble work.

14.7 Coping with Loss: Finding Solace and Strength in Our Beloved's Memory

14.7.1 Grieving and Healing Together

During this difficult time, it is important to remember that we are not alone in our grief. As we mourn the loss of [Name], let us come together to offer support and comfort to one another. Sharing our sorrow, memories, and tears can provide a sense of solace and help ease the pain we feel. Together, we can navigate the journey of grief and find strength in the collective love we shared for [Name].

14.7.2 Finding Comfort in Memories and Shared Stories

In the depths of our sorrow, it is essential to cling to the memories we have of [Name]. Recall the laughter, the joy, and the unforgettable moments spent together. As we share stories and reminisce, we honor [Name]'s life and find solace in the knowledge that [his/her] spirit will forever live on in the cherished memories we hold. Let us find comfort in the love we shared and the impact [Name] had on each of our lives.

14.8.A Final Farewell: Embracing the Legacy and Carrying Our Beloved's Light Forward

14.8.1 Honoring the Legacy and Continuing the Work

As we bid a final farewell to [Name], let us pledge to honor [his/her] legacy by continuing the important work [he/she] started. [Name] touched countless lives and made a difference in the world, and it is now our responsibility to carry [his/her] torch forward. Let [Name]'s passion for change ignite a fire within each of us, propelling us to take action and make a positive impact in our own unique ways.

14.8.2 Keeping the Spirit Alive in Our Hearts

Although [Name] may no longer be physically present, [his/her] spirit will forever reside in our hearts. Let us keep [his/her] memory alive by embodying the qualities that made [Name] so special: kindness, compassion, and a zest for life. Whenever we face challenges or need guidance, let us turn to the lessons [Name] taught us and draw strength from [his/her] enduring legacy. In doing so, we ensure that [Name]'s light continues to shine brightly in our lives.

14.8.B Final Farewell: Embracing the Legacy and Carrying the Light Forward

As we say our final goodbyes to [Name], we are reminded that [his/her] presence in our lives was a true blessing. Though [his/her] time with us was cut short, [Name] leaves behind a legacy of love, laughter, and inspiration that will continue to guide us. Let us honor [Name]'s memory by embracing [his/her] zest for life, embodying the lessons [he/she] taught us, and carrying [his/her] light within our hearts. In this final farewell, we bid adieu to a remarkable soul, grateful for the time we had together and determined to make every moment count, just as [Name] did. Rest in peace, dear [Name], knowing that your beautiful life will never be forgotten.

15. Holding onto Memories and Letting Go with Love

15.1 Introduction: Celebrating the Life and Memories of our Loved Ones

When we lose someone dear to us, the pain of grief can feel overwhelming. However, amidst the sorrow, it is essential to remember that our departed loved ones have left behind a beautiful legacy of memories and experiences. In this reflective chapter, we will explore the process of holding onto those cherished memories while also finding the courage to let go with love. By honoring their journey, embracing grief, and discovering meaningful ways to commemorate their lives, we can navigate the path of healing and discover a sense of peace in our loss. Let us embark on this journey of celebrating the beautiful life of our dearest departed, finding solace in the power of remembrance, and cherishing the present moment with gratitude.

15.1.1 Honoring the Journey of our Departed

As humans, we are blessed to have the capacity to form deep connections with others. When we lose someone dear to us, it can be difficult to navigate the complex emotions that come with grief. However, in the midst of sorrow, it is important to remember that our loved ones had a unique journey that deserves to be celebrated. By honoring their life, we can find comfort in the memories they left behind, and keep their spirit alive in our hearts.

15.1.2 Embracing the Power of Remembrance

Remembrance is a beautiful way to hold onto the precious moments we shared with our departed loved ones. Whether it's a favorite song, a shared hobby, or a cherished memory, these little fragments of the past can bring comfort and solace in times of grief. Embracing the power of remembrance allows us to keep the bond alive and creates a space for connection beyond the physical realm. It's through remembering that we find the strength to heal and continue living, while cherishing the beautiful lives they led.

15.2 Embracing Grief: Understanding the Importance of Grieving and Healing

15.2.1 Acknowledging the Pain of Loss

Grief is a natural response to loss, and it's crucial to acknowledge the pain that comes with it. It is okay to feel a wide range of emotions - sadness, anger, confusion, or even relief. Each person's grief journey is unique, and there is no right or wrong way to grieve. By allowing ourselves to fully experience and express our emotions, we open the door to healing and growth.

15.2.2 Exploring the Different Stages of Grief

Grief is not a linear process, but rather a series of stages that we may move through in our own time. From denial and anger to bargaining, depression, and acceptance, these stages capture the different emotional landscapes we navigate while mourning. It's important to remember that these stages are not fixed, and everyone experiences grief in their own way. By embracing each stage, we can better understand our emotions and give ourselves permission to heal.

15.2.3 Seeking Professional Help and Support

During times of loss, it's essential to reach out for support. Grief can be overwhelming, and having a compassionate professional to guide us through the process can be immensely helpful. Therapists, grief counselors, or support groups provide safe spaces to share our feelings, gain perspective, and learn coping strategies. Surrounding ourselves with understanding and empathetic individuals helps us navigate the difficult journey of grief and find solace in the company of others who have experienced similar losses.

15.3 Honoring Their Legacy: Preserving and Sharing the Memories of our Departed

15.3.1 Collecting and Organizing Cherished Mementos

Mementos and keepsakes can hold tremendous sentimental value. From handwritten notes and photographs to special trinkets that remind us of our loved ones, these tangible items serve as powerful reminders of the moments we shared together. By collecting and organizing these precious mementos, we create a physical representation of their legacy, allowing us to revisit cherished memories whenever we desire.

15.3.2 Creating a Memorial Space

Creating a dedicated memorial space can bring comfort and provide a sacred place for remembrance. Whether it's a small corner adorned with photographs and candles, or a beautiful garden where their presence can be felt, this space becomes a sanctuary where we can go to reflect, connect, and feel close to our departed loved ones. It's a tangible reminder that their memory lives on, and a special place to honor their impact on our lives.

15.3.3 Sharing Stories and Memories with Others

Sharing stories and memories about our departed loved ones is a powerful way to keep their legacy alive. When we share anecdotes, funny incidents, or heartfelt experiences with others, it not only helps us process our grief, but also allows others to know and appreciate the beautiful life that was lived. By sharing stories, we create a sense of connection, ripples of love, and inspire others to remember and celebrate their precious memories as well.

15.4 Letting Go with Love: Embracing Acceptance and Finding Peace in the Loss

15.4.1 Understanding the Concept of Letting Go

Letting go doesn't mean forgetting or erasing the memories of our departed loved ones. Instead, it's about releasing the grip of grief that may hinder our growth and prevent us from finding peace. Letting go is a gradual process of accepting that the physical presence of our loved ones may no longer be with us, but the love and impact they had on our lives will forever remain.

15.4.2 Cultivating Acceptance and Forgiveness

Acceptance can be a challenging aspect of the grieving process. It's about acknowledging that the loss is a part of our reality and that life will never be the same. This acceptance doesn't dismiss the pain we feel, but rather allows us to make peace with it. Additionally, forgiveness plays a crucial role in finding inner peace. By forgiving ourselves and others for any regrets or grievances, we free ourselves from the burden of unresolved emotions and open ourselves up to healing.

15.4.3 Finding Peace and Solace Through Self-Care

Amidst grief, it's important to prioritize self-care. Taking time for ourselves, indulging in activities that bring us joy, and practicing self-compassion can help ease the pain and bring moments of peace. Whether it's spending time in nature, engaging in creative outlets, or seeking solace in the embrace of loved ones, self-care becomes a gentle reminder to nurture ourselves as we navigate the uncharted waters of grief. Remember, it's okay to find moments of happiness and peace even in the midst of mourning.

15.5 Rituals and Memorials: Creating Meaningful Ways to Remember and Commemorate

15.5.1 Exploring Cultural and Religious Rituals

When we lose someone dear to us, exploring the rituals of our cultural or religious background can be a source of comfort and connection. These rituals have been passed down through generations, offering guidance on how to honor and remember our loved ones. Whether it's lighting a candle, saying a prayer, or performing a specific ceremony, these acts can provide a sense of peace and continuity in the midst of grief.

15.5.2 Designing Personalized Memorials and Tributes

In addition to traditional rituals, designing personalized memorials and tributes can be a beautiful way to honor our departed loved ones. From creating a memory wall adorned with photographs and mementos to planting a tree in their memory, the possibilities are as unique as the individuals we are remembering. These personalized gestures can serve as tangible reminders of the love and impact our loved ones had on our lives.

15.5.3 Incorporating Symbolic Gestures and Traditions

Incorporating symbolic gestures and traditions can add depth and meaning to our remembrances. Whether it's releasing butterflies as a symbol of transformation, lighting lanterns to represent the eternal flame of love, or even wearing a specific piece of jewelry that holds significance, these small gestures can help us feel connected to our loved ones even after they have left this world. It's these touches of symbolism that can bring comfort and a sense of spiritual continuity.

15.6 Healing Through Connection: Finding Solace in Community and Support Networks

15.6.1 The Importance of Leaning on Loved Ones

During times of grief, it's crucial to lean on our loved ones for support. Sharing our feelings with those who knew our departed loved ones can provide solace and understanding. Whether it's reminiscing about happy memories or simply having someone to listen, the support of our loved ones can help us navigate the complex emotions that come with loss.

15.6.2 Joining Support Groups and Bereavement Communities

In addition to the support of our immediate circle, joining support groups and bereavement communities can offer a sense of solace and understanding. Connecting with others who have experienced a similar loss can provide a safe space to share our emotions, seek guidance, and find comfort in knowing we are not alone in our grief.

15.6.3 Engaging in Acts of Compassion and Service

Engaging in acts of compassion and service can also be healing during the grieving process. Volunteering our time to help others in need can offer a sense of purpose and fulfillment. By channeling our pain into acts of kindness, we not only honor our departed loved ones but also find healing through the connections we make with others.

15.7 Embracing Life: Emphasizing the Importance of Cherishing the Present Moment

15.7.1 Reflecting on the Impermanence of Life

The loss of a loved one reminds us of the impermanence of life. It serves as a poignant reminder to cherish the moments we have with the people we hold dear. Reflecting on this impermanence can inspire us to live fully and make the most of every precious second.

15.7.2 Finding Joy in Everyday Experiences

Finding joy in everyday experiences becomes even more significant when we are grieving. It's important to take notice of the small moments that bring us happiness and allow ourselves to fully experience them. Whether it's savoring a delicious meal, laughing with friends, or appreciating the beauty of nature, finding joy can help us heal and honor our departed loved ones.

15.7.3 Living a Life that Honors our Departed Loved Ones

One of the most meaningful ways to remember our departed loved ones is by living a life that honors their memory. This means embracing the values, passions, and qualities they held dear. It means carrying their love and wisdom with us, and allowing it to guide us in our decisions and actions. By living in a way that reflects their spirit, we ensure that their memory lives on, forever cherished in our hearts.

As we conclude this heartfelt exploration of holding onto memories and letting go with love, may we carry forward the lessons learned and the love shared with our departed loved ones. Grief is a lifelong journey, but by embracing acceptance, honoring their legacy, and finding solace in community and self-care, we can gradually find healing and peace. Let us continue to celebrate the beautiful lives they lived, cherish the memories they left behind, and live our own lives to the fullest, keeping their spirit alive within us. Though our beloved may be physically gone, their love and impact remain forever etched in our hearts and as we remember those we have lost, let us strive to create a safer and more compassionate world.

Frequently Asked Questions

A. Writing the Eulogy

A.1 Can anyone contribute to the eulogy for our beloved?

Yes, absolutely. The eulogy is an opportunity for friends, family members, and loved ones to share their personal memories and reflections on the deceased's life. If you would like to contribute to the eulogy, reach out to the person organizing the service or the individual designated to speak during the ceremony.

A.2 How long should the eulogy be?

The length of the eulogy can vary depending on the traditions, preferences, and time constraints of the memorial service. Generally, a eulogy is around 5 to 10 minutes long, allowing enough time to capture the essence of the departed's life and impact. However, it is important to remember that quality matters more than quantity. Focus on sharing meaningful stories and heartfelt messages that truly honor your loved one.

A.3 Can I include humor in the eulogy?

Yes, incorporating lighthearted and humorous anecdotes can be a beautiful way to celebrate the joyful moments and unique personality of the departed. However, it is essential to strike a balance and be mindful of the overall tone of the service. Ensure that any humor is respectful and appropriate for the occasion, keeping in mind the feelings of the grieving family and attendees.

A.4 Is it necessary to follow a particular structure for the eulogy?

While there is no one-size-fits-all structure for a eulogy, it is helpful to have a loose outline to guide your speech. Consider including sections such as an introduction, sharing personal memories, highlighting achievements and contributions, discussing the impact on family and loved ones, and concluding with a heartfelt farewell. However, feel free to adapt the structure to best reflect the unique life and relationship you shared with your loved one.

B. The Eulogy and the Healing Process

B.1 Why is delivering a eulogy important in the healing process?

Delivering a eulogy provides an opportunity to express grief, honor the life of the departed, and find solace in shared memories. It allows us to reflect on the impact the person had on our lives and to celebrate their legacy, fostering healing and closure in the grieving process.

B.2 How can I gather memories and stories for a personalized eulogy?

You can gather memories and stories by reaching out to family members, friends, and loved ones who knew the person well. Conduct interviews, ask for personal anecdotes, and encourage others to share their cherished memories. This collaborative approach ensures the eulogy captures the essence of the individual and reflects the collective experiences of those who knew them.

B.3 How do I address the pain and offer comfort in a eulogy?

Addressing the pain and offering comfort in a eulogy can be achieved by acknowledging the difficulties of grief and loss. Share personal reflections on the impact of the death, express empathy towards others who are mourning, and offer words of comfort, hope, and healing. The eulogy should create a space for collective healing and provide solace to those in attendance.

B.4 What if I find it difficult to write a tribute or express my emotions through words?

Writing a tribute can be challenging, especially when emotions are overwhelming. Take your time and be gentle with yourself. Consider seeking support from others, such as close friends or family members, who can help you brainstorm ideas or even write the tribute together. Alternatively, you can explore other forms of expression like art, music, or creating a visual collage to honor your loved one.

B.5 What role do rituals and symbolism play in a meaningful eulogy?

Rituals and symbolism can add depth and meaning to a eulogy. Consider incorporating rituals, such as lighting candles, sharing symbolic objects, or inviting others to contribute to a memory jar. These gestures can create a sense of sacredness, foster connection, and provide an opportunity for mourners to actively participate in the healing process.

C. Honoring and Preserving and Memories

C.1 How can I honor the memory of a loved one who passed away suddenly?

There are various ways to honor the memory of a loved one lost suddenly. You can create a memorial or tribute, such as a photo album, a dedicated webpage, or a charitable foundation in their name. Engaging in activities or causes that were important to your loved one can also serve as a meaningful way to honor their legacy. Additionally, sharing stories and memories with others can help keep their spirit alive.

C.2 How can I preserve memories in a meaningful way?

Preserving memories can be achieved through various methods. Some common strategies include writing in journals, creating scrapbooks or photo albums, making digital archives, and recording videos. Choose a method that resonates with you and allows you to capture and cherish the memories in a way that feels most meaningful.

D. Grieving and Moving On

D.1 How can I cope with the sudden loss of a loved one?

Coping with sudden loss can be an overwhelming and challenging experience. It is important to allow yourself to grieve and feel the full range of emotions. Seek support from friends, family, or a therapist who can provide comfort and guidance during this difficult time. Engaging in self-care activities, such as exercise, journaling, or spending time in nature, can also help in the healing process.

D.2 How can I find solace and joy amidst the sorrow of losing someone?

Finding solace and joy amidst sorrow is a personal journey, but there are several strategies that may help. Embracing joyful remembrance by focusing on happy memories and cherished moments can bring comfort. Engaging in activities that celebrate their life, such as creating personalized tributes or participating in rituals of remembrance, can also help in finding solace and healing.

D.3 Is it normal to feel a mix of emotions when grieving the loss of someone?

Absolutely. Grief is a complex and individual experience. It is entirely normal to feel a wide range of emotions, including sadness, anger, guilt, or even moments of joy, hope and even optimism when reminiscing about the person's life. These emotions can stem from the love and connection shared with the departed, as well as from a desire to honor their memory. It is important to give yourself permission to feel and process these emotions in your own time and in your own way.

D.4 How can I navigate the grieving process with the support of my community?

Seeking support from your community can be incredibly helpful during the grieving process. Reach out to family, friends, or support groups who can provide a listening ear and understanding. Sharing stories and memories, attending memorial services, or participating in community events can foster a sense of belonging and provide comfort in knowing that you are not alone in your grief.

D.5 How can I keep the memory of my loved one alive while moving forward with my own life?

Keeping the memory of your loved one alive is a personal and ongoing process. Find ways to honor their legacy by engaging in activities or causes that were important to them. Consider creating rituals or traditions that commemorate their life, such as annual memorial gatherings or participating in activities they enjoyed. Additionally, finding ways to incorporate their values and teachings into your life can keep their spirit alive while also allowing you to move forward and find hope.

D.6 How can memories help in the grieving process?

Memories play a crucial role in the grieving process by allowing us to connect with the essence of our loved ones. They serve as a source of comfort, healing, and inspiration. Memories provide a way to honor the lives of those we have lost, keeping their spirit alive in our hearts.

D.7 Is it beneficial to share memories with others who have experienced a similar loss?

Absolutely. Sharing memories with others who have gone through a similar loss can create a supportive community, providing empathy, understanding, and validation. It allows for the exchange of stories, experiences, and emotions, providing comfort and a sense of connection in the midst of grief.

D.8 What can I do to support someone who is grieving?

Offering support to someone who is grieving can make a significant difference in their healing process. Be present, listen without judgment, and provide a safe space for them to express their emotions. Offer practical help, such as assisting with funeral arrangements or everyday tasks. Most importantly, respect their unique grieving process and be patient with their journey.

D.9 How can I cope with my own grief while supporting others?

Coping with your own grief while supporting others can be challenging. It is essential to establish healthy boundaries, prioritize self-care, and seek support from friends, family, or professionals. Practice active listening and empathy, but also allow yourself the space to grieve. Remember that supporting others does not mean neglecting your own healing process. Seek a balance between comforting others and taking care of yourself.

www.ingramcontent.com/pod-product-compliance
Lightning Source LLC
Chambersburg PA
CBHW030022290326
41934CB00005B/449